MAJESTIC EXPRESSIONS

SCRIBBLINGS FROM THE DEPTHS

ANU ABRAHAM

Copyright © Anu Abraham
All Rights Reserved.

This book has been published with all efforts taken to make the material error-free after the consent of the author. However, the author and the publisher do not assume and hereby disclaim any liability to any party for any loss, damage, or disruption caused by errors or omissions, whether such errors or omissions result from negligence, accident, or any other cause.

While every effort has been made to avoid any mistake or omission, this publication is being sold on the condition and understanding that neither the author nor the publishers or printers would be liable in any manner to any person by reason of any mistake or omission in this publication or for any action taken or omitted to be taken or advice rendered or accepted on the basis of this work. For any defect in printing or binding the publishers will be liable only to replace the defective copy by another copy of this work then available.

Dedicated to: My Parents,

*Dr. Rekha Dayal, Mrs. Harsha Kuldeep, and
Kiran Sachdeva*

Contents

Preface

Many of us go through several experiences, emotions and feelings in our daily life. Some people wish to express those feelings by giving a creative form to them and it is indeed a blessing if one is able to do so. I feel that sense of being blessed when I see that I am able to give wings to my expressions in the form of this book. This book titled " Majestic Expressions" is a collection of 18 poems. Each poem in the book may give you a different vibe, a distinct feeling, as it is written on several themes and topics, some fanciful and others very close to our real lives. I hope it would help the readers to go through a range of varied emotions, which they too might have went through in their lives, at some point or the other.

Happy Reading....

Anu Abraham

Acknowledgements

First and foremost, I would like to thank God Almighty for blessing me with this passion for writing. Without the Divine blessings, I wouldn't have been able to accomplish this task. I would also like to thank my family, my friends, and all those people who are connected with me in one way or the other.

I feel grateful that I am able to complete this book which has a collection of 18 poems written by me.

I once again wholeheartedly thank everyone for supporting me at each point in my life.

I would also like to specially thank my teacher Late Mrs Vimala R for always supporting me and for giving me all the lessons i needed for life. "Though you are not with me in person, i always feel your love and blessings".

I would also want to thank my mom's paternal uncle, Late Prof. P C Alias, who was more like a grandfather for me. Being an amazing writer, and orator, he was my inspiration to try penning down my feelings. "Thank you Chacha for showering your love and blessings on me".

Again, Special Thanks to: Dr.Rekha Dayal, Mrs.Harsha Kuldeep and Kiran Sachdeva for always encouraging me.

Also, Special Thanks to: Archana Midhun, Kamyaa Wadhwa, Sanyukta Karmarkar, Shalu George, Shibu George, My cute princess Jianna, Swati Rose Thomas, and Asha Satish for always cheering me up with positive vibes.

About The Publisher

Notion Press is a global platform for anyone who believes in the power of words and the impact it can have on the world we live in. Our vision is to help every aspiring writer give their idea an identity, a tangible form and a medium to spread it. In our quest to redefine the publishing space, we constantly strive to innovate and evolve the publishing process. Our publishing platform enables writers to convert their stories and ideas into books that people can hold, read and connect with.

Notion Press started on January 1, 2012 as a provider of high quality publishing services to authors in India. Today, Notion Press offers various publishing, book printing and distribution options to both authors and publishers from around the world. We are a technology start-up & one of the fastest growing book publishing companies in India that aims to solve problems in book publishing and distribution by creating highly scalable solutions that work across the globe.

ABOUT THE PUBLISHER

About The Author

Anu Abraham is a young budding writer. A girl born in Kerala and bought up in Delhi, she has been very fond of reading and writing since childhood. She recollects her memories of reading short story books while traveling in train whenever she goes for a vacation in Kerala. Anu has completed her schooling from Kerala School, Vikaspuri, New

Delhi. Further she did her graduation from Jesus and Mary College, University of Delhi. She has also done B.Ed. from Maharishi Dayanand University. She believes that when pen and passion come together, the result is a beautiful creation. This ideology inspired her to write poetry, essay, short story, etc.

She has a keen passion towards writing and equally interested to write both in English and Hindi language. Her write ups in both the languages have already been published in several anthologies. She has also compiled a Hindi Anthology titled" Maa: Naaritv ka Anootha Roop" Anu is a person who seldom looks forward to groom her skills to the maximum. She has a desire to inspire many young minds through her writings. She gives the credit of every achievement and every happiness in her life to her beloved teachers. She says that without the support and constant encouragement from her teachers, her writings would have been locked up in some shelf.

1. My Lifeline..

Just as the night is incomplete

Without the stars and moonlight,

And the day is insignificant

Without the glowing sunlight,

In the absence of your pure love

My life will become deserted and

I will be worthless and deficient.

You are brighter than the sunlight

You alone can light up

my face with a smile,

You are pleasing than the soft winds

You alone can turn my life into a bliss,

You are beautiful than the springs

You alone can inspire this young mind,

You are prettier than blooming flowers

You touch my heart with your soft words,

You are amazing than all wonders

The very reason for my existence,

You are more than anything for me

For you I will give everything of mine,

There's only a desire in my life

To be your beloved one throughout.

2. Golden Memories

Some old books in the shelf,
The broken brushes, colorful bottles,
Yet some torn paper pieces;
They remind me the precious
Times, that I long for now.

Those were the real days,
Without worries and fears;
All of us in the same shades,
With new vibrant bags and umbrellas,
In the green patchy school yard.

It's a feeling, that nothing could replace;
The early morning lessons,
Those chirpy chatting of ours,
And all the playful moments within,
Our clean n clumsy classrooms.

The carpet of dust in the ground,
Felt like hot deserts in the summers,
The same ground, disguises itself,

To a brownish mud pond,
During the days of slippery rains;

Yet another fond memory is,
Of the vivid fragrant flowers,
And of those rusty benches,
Where we used to sit at peace,
Gazing eagerly at the passers.

I wish I could get back those days,
Once again to live in the ways,
I used to, as carefree as a bird,
As joyful as a butterfly
And hop around in that same yard.

3. The Empty Cradle

Mom can you hear me
I am your little baby girl,
Why You don't make me sleep
In your soft and loving lap,
Why are you not feeding me
With your comfy hands.

She suddenly opened her eyes
Looked around and thought,
"My child would be longing for me"
She felt as if she could hear,
Only the voice of the little one so dear
In that melancholically dark night.

She too was longing for a sight
Of her baby who is no more with her,
She just looked onto the cradle lying there
It just reminded her of the cute smiles,
And the sweet giggling voice
That her little one would produce.

She used to look at her and smile
Seeing her angelic face was a pile,
Of joy, content and happiness
But now all around its an emptiness,
A grave sorrow engulfing her
After all, she is a mother.

She carried her little one in her womb
For several months,
Endured all the pain and gave her
All the love and care before seeing her,
Now how can she accept the truth
That her young doll is gone
Gone forever, never to return.

How she could believe
That the life which was a part,
Of her flesh and Soul
Had gone so soon so far,
She cried, screamed in agony
And cursed the world's powers,
After all, she is a mother.

As she was still craving
To hug her child tight,

Give her lots of kisses at night
Make her sleep with melodious lullabies,
She wanted to be her shadow
As her young one took each footsteps.

But dismay and grief took place of hopes
All her wishes were burnt into ashes,
She begged to the universe
To bring her little one back, but in vain,
All she could do was to be a puppet
To the game of heartless destiny.

4. A Battle Unresolved

He the Creator made us all alike
We all got divided with dislike,
Towards shades and colors
That seemed different or lower,
Than we could see in our own self.

Why is that we are so forgetful
Why is it that we don't realize,
We are the visitors of few days
The moment our tickets expire,
We all are back to the same soil
Where all shades are equal.

Why is it that we consider
Another person to be inferior
Just because he or she has a shade lower,
Why is it that we can't understand
Its just a matter of mere skin tones,
Rest all are nothing but mortal persons.

What is the difference that we find
That we keep away our fellow men
And make them feel so embarrassed?
Why is it that we can't see
The fair or dark tones of today
Will fade away some day?
And all our deeds on Earth,
Are the only shades that will stay.

Why is it that even young minds
Have the vulgarity to make fun
Based on looks and colours?
And again why is it that the adults too
Do the same thing throughout
Without even a second thought.

Have all the hearts gone ruthless
Have all the souls became gruesome?
Why is it that we don't think
Even for a moment,
What we show and teach today
Will only be the pillars of our future.

If we teach them the power
Of hate based on fair and dark,
We are going to find ourselves
In the real dark, when old age comes,
As the fair tones and shades are not static
They fade away and leave us as time goes by.

Then the rough game would start
When the poison we spread once
Starts to choke and kill ourselves,
Lets give it a thought calmly and deeply
What we want in store for us,
The sweetness of mankind
Or the bitterness of brutal hate.

5. A Paladin

Snow covered mountains and patches
And some men in similar attires
They were standing aloof and rigid,
With guns and ammunitions fully loaded
Surrounded by arms and tankers,
Yes, that's what you get to see at the borders.

At times I think, how is it possible
To have such an utmost dedication
A sheer readiness to be sacrificed,
I heard an inner voice that told
Each one is a paladin, there
The brave hearted sons of the Mother.

They stand there ready to get beheaded
Ensuring that none on Earth dare
To harm the sanctity and rectitude,
Of their motherland, so beloved
Each one there have taken the oath,
To guard the kids of the Mother.

Again I thought, they too might
Have a family of four or eight
Old parents who gave birth to them,
A young, new bride who came
To be a part of their life and home
And even a little champ for whom,
Each one there is a superhero.

They wait, at least, once in a year
To meet that person, very dear
But the very sight of a military van,
With flowers, obituary posters and army men
Surely shatters them all to the core,
But still they don't shed a drop of tear.

I heard the youngest one saying
We can't dishonour him by crying
He is my dad, afterall, a brave man,
The moment I came across these words
A sense of respect started flowing,
And filled my heart with gratitude.

How brave must be that lady
Whose hopes and dreams dashed
She wished to sail till the end,
But couldn't even spend
Some moments together with him,

As he left, just after tying the knot.

And what must be going through
The hearts of the little ones there
Who were waiting for gifts, so excited,
But got to see their dad in a coffin instead,
And received in hand a folded flag
Heard in the air repeated gun shots,
As his fellow army men paid tribute.

I thought, it must be hard for the aged ones
To see their beloved gone much before them
Yes its indeed hard, we can't be them,
We can't live like them nor even think
Of it, even for a micro second's blink,
To all those bravehearts of the land,
My heart gives a salute, not merely by hand.

6. The Supersonic Age

The pace is so much fast
All are rushing past the other
No one has the time for another,
Why this extra haste after all?
Why have people become
Mere switches at work,
Just like machines at task?

The couples don't care
To spend with each other,
They say they are busy
With work not so easy,
How is it that they got
Time to tie a knot ?

Parents, also don't care
To talk with their children,
They too say they are
Busy with their office burden,
How is it that they got
Time to form a zygote ?

Children don't have to care
For the parents so old,
They say they have work
For which they have to be hard,
How is it that they got
Time to spent with friends out?

No one has time for someone
All have become so clueless,
Where all of them are going ?
What all are they chasing ?
It seems as if people are there
But without the feel of being here.

Are they getting time to eat,
Or are they running on empty fuel?
Are they able to sleep at night,
Or are they learning to wake all time?
Are they getting time to breathe,
Or are they lifeless machines ?

They all are after something bigger
Which they feel are more better,
Seeing all this it feels terrible
And a voice deep from heart told,
The old times were more beautiful.

Although it didn't have everything
At the click of a finger,
But it does had the charm of life,
The slow pace of life was good
Which had a feel of love and care for all,
But now its like a crowded town
Yet all deserted and alone.

7. Humans Indeed

We are born into the species
Known worldwide as humans,
We live our life like humans only
But are we so from inside really;

A poor man or a woman
Begs on the street to live,
We close our eyes to them
And get busy in our own riches,
Yes, we are humans indeed;

Another old man shivers in cold
And several kids lying on the roadside,
From where you and me daily ride
Yet they remain un-noticed,
Yes, we are humans indeed;

We may get to see,
The pitiful and shameful sight of a girl,
Getting molested right in front, but
Our ears are dysfunctional and closed
To the piercing voice of her screams,
Yes, we are humans indeed;

A fellow man may be bleeding
Begging to save his life on the same road,
And we simply rush past that man
Pretending we haven't heard,
Yes, we are humans indeed;

An unruly van may come on that road
And harshly take away the young child,
Just as an Eagle catches its prey
Yet we seem to be cool and unaffected,
Yes, we can say, we are humans indeed;

We may also come across a tiny bird
With wounds on its wings,
Unable to fly, struggling hard,
It may even happen, it gets killed
By some vehicle running on the road,

Yes, we are humans indeed;

So many things happen around
But our senses are deliberately closed,
We prefer not to interfere
And not to take a step forward,
After all, we are humans indeed;

A question arises here in my thought
Or I would say, made me wondered,
What would be going on in His mind
The one who made us all in his form,
Maybe He Himself would be shocked
Have I really made Humans indeed.

8. Withered Out

Young little innocent souls,
Wandering on roads,
Thrown out of homes,
Left at busy streets,
Even abandoned mercilessly,
At the railway tracks,
Or gates of orphanages;

And I wonder what's going on,
What wrong they might have done,
Have they taken a birth
Just to suffer on this Earth,
How the destiny can be so cruel?
That it made their lives a hell;

So many questions unsolved,
Revolving in my mind, so shattered,
By the glimpse of recklessness,
Of both man and nature around,
How are those little caterpillars

Going to safely survive,
Fighting off all the odds,
Of this sharp and crooked world;

Its not one, nor few nor many ,
There are millions of them,
Who lose out a chance to live,
Even before starting the journey,
Yes, there are several of them,
Whose little hopes and silly dreams ,
Are withered out,
Even before they start to bloom.

9. A Boon Gone Forever

Time, is supreme in power
Flowing, like an unstoppable river,
Whether we rise or fall, it wont care,
Once it's gone, is gone forever;

Is it the human err or fate,
That we can't enjoy this precious gift
And then again to look for and wait,
For the wind to come back,
Come once more in our right;

Why is it that we rush and go away,
Never valuing the miracles in our way,
And then why do we cry and say,
That they soon vanished away?

Yet we wait amidst the ambiguity
Never knowing the reality,
That time was a boon indeed,
Which once gone, is gone forever
Laughing at us with a pity;

Are we really worth of the stars,
Or are we still slithering on ground?
Just to create some lasting scars,
And never to heal the gnawing wound;

I wonder at times of creation,
Of the strangeness of the destiny,
Where it takes us, to heaven or to hell,
And what it has kept in store for all,
As we move on with the tide and sail.

10. The Cruise

The Cruise is still on its voyage
Amidst the waves that enrage,
But it just has to manage
And reach the other side,
Safe and sound, no matter what.

In this journey of uncertainty
Each one is a captain,
Every step has to lead to destiny
Or else the Cruise will drown,
Into the depths very soon.

Some days the winds stay calm
Yet on other days it may be sharp,
The waves too may turn in fury
And may dwindle the hopes,
But yet the captain has to sail on.

There are some people in the ship
Some sweet, some sour and,
Yet others so cunning and bitter,

It's so exhausting to carry them along,
But yet the captain has to sail on.

Looking for the wind's direction
He has to be alert of the water,
As if it enters the cruise and fills in
Then he can't save the cruise,
It's a huge risk and a big task,
But yet the captain has to sail on.

He too may be confused to the core
Surrounded by worries of all sort,
Maybe haunted by memories, so sore,
And even broken from deep inside,
But yet he's the captain, he has to sail on.

11. The Banyan Tree

There stood the banyan tree
At the riverside corner,
It looked so majestic and carefree
As if it had witnessed almost all life's miser.

It seemed as if the tree was a century old
But yet so excited with its hanging wings,
It may have some burried gold,
Beneath its soil,
and even other precious things.

It has given many evenings
Of calm and cheer to the old and young,
It has given a million mornings,
Of fresh air to everyone passing.

The tree had a different charm and beauty
Adding an elegance to the place's bounty,
It also had some bad name of being ghosty,
As there spread some stories of vampires at night.

All through the day, it gets company of many
But once, the moon comes up and,
The earth gets covered by the dark blanket,
Not even a single man paases that way.

The tree too feels so strange and lonely
That the people who enjoy its shade during the day,
Get afraid of a blood thirsty ghost,
Whom the tree itself had never met.

Sometimes the tree might have really felt
To sit and chit chat with that whimsical ghost,
Atleast, it can get rid off the loneliness,
Or it can request the ghost to sing along,
Its hanging wings,as the wind strikes them.

As Being a tree, so old and mature
It may feel equal pleasure and happiness,
Or may not feel any peculiar difference,
On talking with a human or even a vampire.

12. My Special Love

If Love is the sweetness of life,
Then you are my sweet flower,
If care is the magic in life,
Then you are a magical wand.
If trust is the light of life,
Then you are my brightest light.
If friendship is the warmth of life,
Then you are my warm blanket.
If affection is the comfort of life,
Then you are my best comfort zone.
If being true is the way to best life,
Then you are my righteous path.
If kindness is the fruit of life,
Then you are the best fruit of taste.
If goodness is the virtue of life,
Then you are my passion.
And I shall follow your path.

13. Is it a Big Deal?

Meet her, she is a girl, a daughter
As soft as a flower,
The best secret keeper
The perfect care taker,
Her day starts even before the sun
And ends after the rise of the moon,
You may not feel it as a big deal
As its her duty, of being a girl.

She is one, yet is in many roles
She knows about each one,
May it be the cup of tea in the morning
Or the crispy snacks of the evening,
Her hands reach each corner of the house
Again it's not a very big deal
She is doing her duty of being a girl.

She may have a million dreams
And she may sacrifice all of them
Not for her, but for her own people,
Then she is the only one with her

To console her broken heart,
Again it's not a big deal
As she will learn to adjust, as she is a girl.

She never says anything to anyone
But does someone even bother to hear?
The vicious circle of so called gender roles
Has taken away even her identity
But yes, she has to silently suffer,
Even the burning flames quietly
It's not a big deal, as she is a girl.

Try to have a look into her heart
You may get to see a pile
Of unheard voices, hopes and dreams,
Which she used to cherish
And she didn't knew then,
She had only option, one identity
That she has to be like a girl,
Again it's not a big deal.

But at times she feels to lash out
To explode her anger and fury,
At times she feel so suffocated
And her soul dies from within,
When you say she is only a girl,

she is to be someone else's
We need a son for our lineage.

Is it really a Big Deal?

14. The Canvas

The painting is so adorable
With colors, so beautiful,
The whole canvas is filled,
With different marvelous shades,
Its just a beautiful masterpiece,
Said each one, as they saw the art;

Each shade given, each color filled
In it, had a meaning, deep hidden,
Looking closely, Into it, I realized,
It wasn't a mere blue, green and red,
Rather a whole portrait of hopes
Of some precious and pure dreams
Cherished by an innocent soul, so young,
Who looks forward to fly high
With those dreams in its wings;

It had in it, a color of love,
a color of peace and harmony,
A color of joy, a color of hope,
A color of happiness and energy,

But not all can see them clearly
It can pour deep only into a crazy mind,
Eager and passionate to find,
The jewels and diamonds of life.

15. The Dark Day

I woke up one day for a new start
As usual to work for my passion,
I just closed my eyes to remember
The day before, how it went and
What new to do on this new day.

And I could hear those words that
My mother would say to me; my dear girl
You are too ambitious, go ahead
I am sure; one day you will hold
In your hand; the stars of success.

I opened my eyes and looked around
Only to see my dear mother sitting
In front of the flashing flames and
Hot tears flowing down her cheeks
As she saw in front of her, the brutal sight.

The unexpected disaster; the biggest crash
Of her entire life; to witness her
Dear little one burning into ashes

And I was shocked, I asked myself,
Am I dreaming, how could it happen.

Then I realised that my life was over
It got finished at the cruel wish
Of some cold blooded and gruesome hands
They burnt me-my life; my body
Were they so merciless; that they killed
My dreams, hopes and my desires
And to just name it a 'tragedy'.

I wished to live, wanted to fly up high
But they put a fullstop on my life
What wrong I did to them
That those monsters tored me
As if I was a toy at their hands.

I haven't even seen the beauties of life
That they destroyed me and pushed me
Into the never ending darkness
Why? Why they did this to me?
Just because I am a girl; like a lamb
Who couldn't defend a group of wolves.

And yet there are some, at the top
Of luxuries and leisures, they say
It was not the fault of those

Sadistic and blood-thirsty hounds
But my looks evoked them.

I have one thing to ask; only one
To those who justify them; and
To the so called society who
Always frame a conduct code for us
And try to shut us up in a cage.

Would you have reacted the same way
Said the same rules and codes;
Of the so called sanctity and reputation
If it would have happened with
One among you or with one of your own ?

16. A Woman

If you want to see the beauty of the world

Look into the glowing eyes of a woman,

If you want to feel the goodness in the world

Look deep into the heart of a woman,

If you want to know the greatest power

Look into the character of a woman,

If you want to see the world's best creation

Just, look at all of them around you,

Each one of them is a warrior and saviour

Fighting millions of odds that none may know,

Yes, every woman is a super power

Every woman is a blessing on Earth.

17. Beauty of Relations

Relations are not fragile
They are just tender,
The more you pour
Trust and love,
It gets more stronger;

Relations are not difficult
They just need patience,
At times you may need
No utterance to know
Your loved one's heart,
And there are times
Even a million words
Won't take you to the depths;

Relations are not burdens
They just need space,
As you care for one another
The more you try to know

The more amazing it gets;

Relations are not hidden
They just get swayed back,
As we gear up,
In the busyness of life,
They just need some time
Time to show that you care,
To show that you are there.

18. Thoughts..

The world is full of fallacies
No matter how hard we trust,
It only knows to make us fall,
Into the dark pits of grief;
The more we try to move,
It pulls us back rigorously,
Making us doubt our own soul.

No, they can't be changed
They are the most ironical,
Making the crooked reach the top
And degrading the pure souls.

I don't know till when it will be so
When will they learn to be true,
When will they be real?
Or is it that they will never be good
Or rather are we wrong to be good?

There sits a desperate human
Full of dilemmas, unclear truths,
And remains of unfulfilled life;
With a single question striking again
Will anything be nice ever,
Or the destiny is like this, so cruel?